Dwayne's Guitar Lessons presents:

Acoustic Guitar 101

By

Guitar Teacher
Dwayne Jenkins

Tritone publishing © 2025

Copyright © Dwayne Jenkins.
All rights reserved.
Published By Tritone Publishing.

Introduction

When it comes to learning something new, it can sometimes be a bit frustrating. New information to process, new activities to master. How very true this is when it comes to playing the guitar.

That is why I created Acoustic Guitar 101. A comprehensive training course for those looking to get started. There are so many things you need to know and do, it can be overwhelming.

Well, not anymore. This beginner's guidebook leads you confidently along the journey of acoustic guitar playing. It shows you, in a simple step-by-step format, the fundamental principles you need to get started having fun playing the guitar.

Even if you've had no previous music training, or have no previous music knowledge. You can do it with the help of this trusty little companion.

You start out learning about the guitar and the proper way to hold it. You then learn about what each hand is supposed to be doing and how to do it. You then learn how to tune the guitar in a simple, easy fashion that you could do blindfolded.

You then proceed to use a guitar pick and learn about why it is a good idea to get started with one. By this time, you're ready to start having fun.

Introduction

I mean having fun by learning the next lesson, basic guitar chords. I'm not talking about ones that are hard to play, I'm talking about chords you'll find in hundreds of your favorite songs. You will learn how to form them and make them sound like music.

You'll then learn about how to create rhythm and timing, and this is where the guitar starts to come to life. By this time, you'll have your friends saying, "Wow, what song is that?" all from a few chords you learned from this book.

You will learn how to read simple guitar notation so you can easily reference the chords and techniques you learn. You will also learn how to play with your fingers for an even more interesting sound.

Yep, it's all right here. Acoustic Guitar 101. An easy-to-understand guidebook that will have you playing guitar in no time. You'll even learn a little bit of theory, too. Won't that be a hoot? But in such a way, it doesn't come across like a foreign language.

You'll also learn some tips on how to play by ear and practice habits that will get you started right. So, if you want to get started learning to play the guitar today, get your guitar, turn the page and you my friend will be on your way.

Dwayne Jenkins 3/2025

Tritone Publishing © 2025

Contents

Chapter 1: Getting Started 1

Lesson 1: Guitar anatomy 1
Lesson 2: Holding the guitar 3
Chapter 1: Summary 5

Chapter 2: Tuning Up & Using A Pick 7

Lesson 3: Tuning the guitar 7
Lesson 4: Using a pick 9
Chapter 2: Summary 11

Chapter 3: Reading Notation 13

Lesson 5: Chord charts 13
Lesson 6: Guitar tabs 15
Chapter 3: Summary 17

Chapter 4: Forming Basic Chords 19

Lesson 7: Major chords 19
Lesson 8: Minor chords 21
Chapter 4: Summary 23

Chapter 5: Establishing Rhythm 25

Lesson 9: Strumming chords 25
Lesson 10: Develop proper timing 27
Chapter 5: Summary 29

Contents
continued

Chapter 6: Chord Transitions 31
Lesson 11: Changing chords smoothly 31
Lesson 12: Building muscle memory 33
Chapter 6: Summary 35

Chapter 7: More Common Chords 37
Lesson 13: 7th chords 37
Lesson 14: Additional chords 39
Chapter 7: Summary 41

Chapter 8: Capo & Fingerstyle 43
Lesson 15: Using a capo 43
Lesson 16: Using your fingers 45
Chapter 8: Summary 47

Chapter 9: Basic Music Theory 49
Lesson 17: Notes on the fretboard 49
Lesson 18 Chord construction 51
Chapter 9: Summary 53

Chapter 10: Additional Training 55
Lesson 19: Ear training 55
Lesson 20: Practice habits 57
Chapter 10: Summary 59

Acoustic Guitar 101 Conclusion 61

Tritone Publishing © 2025

Chapter 1

Getting Started

Lesson 1: Guitar anatomy

Welcome to Acoustic Guitar 101. This will be a brief course to get you started quickly and easily. When it comes to learning an instrument, the acoustic guitar is a great place to start. It is lightweight and portable, and a starter can be purchased inexpensively.

So, like any good craftsman, we want to make sure we know our tools of the trade. In our case, it is the acoustic guitar. Let's take a look at what it's all about.

Acoustic guitar anatomy:

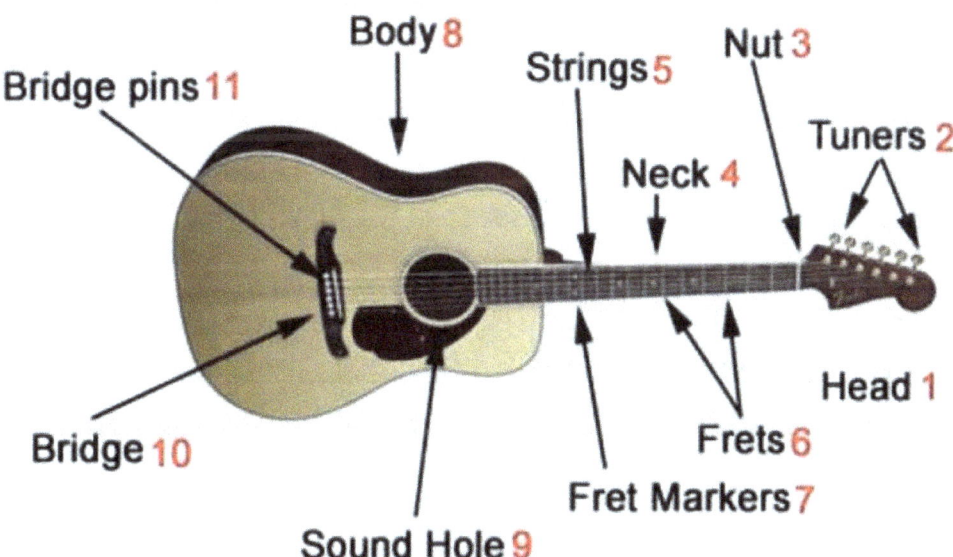

Lesson 1 con't

Headstock: An area for the tuners that hold the strings on.

Tuners: These allow you to adjust the string's tension to a certain pitch.

Nut: A slot that the strings go through and stay separated.

Neck: Holds the nut, fretboard, frets, markers, strings, and head.

Strings: These vibrate at a certain pitch and create sound.

Frets: These allow you to quickly change the pitch of the strings.

Fret markers: These determine where you are along the fretboard.

Body: This attaches the strings to the bridge across the sound hole.

Soundhole: This picks up the string vibration to create sound.

Bridge: Anchors the strings to the guitar body.

Bridge pins: These hold the strings in place on the bridge.

Study the diagram and get familiar with the guitar. Since you're going to be spending time learning to make beautiful music with it, you'll need to get to know it. The better you know it, the better guitar player you will become.

Lesson 2: Holding the guitar

Now that we've been introduced and gotten to know a little bit about the guitar, we can learn how to hold it. This can be done in two ways. Sitting down and standing up. To learn to play it, I recommend you play it sitting down.

Make sure that you are comfortable. The body should be on your lap, and you should be able to wrap one hand around the body, and your other hand should be able to reach the whole fretboard.

Your fretboard hand will be used to form chords, and your picking hand will be used for strumming chords and creating rhythm.

As you can see from the pictures above, you want to make sure that you are relaxed and can reach every part of the guitar easily. The more comfortable you are with the guitar in your hand, the easier it will become to play it.

Lesson 2 con't

In addition to holding the whole guitar, it is a good idea to take a closer look at how each hand should be in position for best performance.

Both should be relaxed while caressing the guitar and be able to easily move about the instrument.

The fretboard hand:

As you can see from the picture, this hand will need the fingers to come up from underneath while the thumb curls over the top of the neck. To get sound out of the guitar, you will need to firmly press down on the strings while forming chords.

The picking hand:

As you can see from the picture, the picking hand should be relaxed and able to strum across all six strings, as well as pick all six individually. This position should feel comfortable. This is very important for creating rhythm and developing timing.

Work on getting your hands to feel relaxed in these positions, as they will be in them while playing the guitar.

Tritone Publishing © 2025

Summary
Chapter 1

In Chapter 1, we have learned some very important aspects. We looked at the guitar anatomy. Parts of the acoustic guitar. This lesson gives us insight into how the guitar works and what makes it tick.

Vibrating six strings across a wooden box with a soundhole. Who knew such an invention would become so popular? I highly recommend that you take time and get familiar with your guitar and all the parts that make it what it is.

From the headstock to the tuners, guitar neck, fretboard, fret markers, bridge, and saddle. All these things make up one of the funniest instruments in the world to play. If you stick with the training, you will see it to be true.

We then learn about how to hold the guitar, and what our two hands should be doing. This is our first step into a great new world. Once we get that guitar in our hands, we began to make it part of us. We began to make a connection with it.

Our fretboard hand will form the chords, and our picking hand will create the rhythm and bring the chords to life. Make them sound like wonderful, wonderful music.

Tritone Publishing © 2025

Chapter 2
Tuning up & Using a pick

Lesson 3: Tuning the guitar

When you tune the guitar you adjust the pitch of the strings. Tighten the string and the pitch goes up, loosen the string and the pitch goes down. When tuning your guitar you will tune it to what is known as standard tuning.

The strings are numbered 1 through 6. You can easily remember this by the thickness of the strings. The biggest string is the highest number, and the thinnest string is the lowest number. The strings also have names, and you will tune the guitar to these names.

String names and numbers are as such:

6th string is Low E (the thickest string)
5th string is A
4th string is D
3rd string is G
2nd string is B
1st string is high E (the smallest string)

**Remember these names because it is what you are going to tune the strings to.

Lesson 3 con't

Now that we know what we're going to tune the guitar strings to, we need to learn how to do it. The best way is with an electronic tuner. The most popular one is the kind that clips onto your guitar headstock.

A clip on tuner   **A clip on tuner attached to the guitar**

As you can see from the pictures, this is what the tuner looks like and how it works attached to your guitar. It has a large display so you can see what the strings are tuned to. Remember, from the thickest string to the smallest, the tuning will be E, A, D, G, B, and E again.

This one is a bit different, but it works the same way. You tighten or loosen the strings until they display the correct letter that corresponds to the string you are tuning. These are great tools to have and will keep your guitar easily in tune.

These tuners will come with instructions on how to use them. They are fairly simple, but I suggest you watch YouTube for more help if you have any issues.

Tritone Publishing © 2025

Lesson 4: Using a pick

When startig out, I recommend you use a guitar pick. The reason for this is because t gives you a more pronounced sound when you strum and pick the strings.

Here are some samples of guitar picks:

Guitar picks come in different colors, textures, and sizes. I recommend you try a few out to see which one works best for you.

Once you decide on the type of pick that feels good, you want to learn how to hold it. This is usually done with the thumb and first finger.

One thing that is great about learning to play guitar is that it is a very personal journey of self discovery that you go on.

As you head down this journey, you'll be doing things you never thought were possible, and that, my friend, can be a very rewarding thing to accomplish.

Taking time to find the right guitar pick will make a huge difference in your playing, so don't overlook this lesson.

Lesson 4 con't

Like I said before, once you find the pick you like, you need to learn to hold it properly. This will allow you to strum across the strings and pick them individually.

The following picture shows you how to hold the guitar pick. The thumb is over the top with your index finger bent underneath and the pointy end sticking out. This will allow you to get the best sound possible out of the guitar strings.

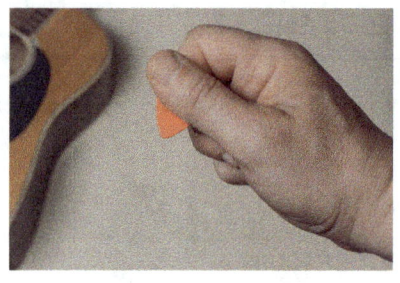

This picture gives a nice view of the guitar pick in use. The arm is across the body, the pick is in place, and striking the strings.

Notice that the pick is facing slightly up. Hold the pick and get used to the movement of strumming down across all six strings.

If you practice daily with a guitar pick, it will help you to develop an articulate percussive attack upon the strings. This will help produce a more precise playing method, and you will get a much brighter sound.

Holding and maneuvering a pick requires coordination between the thumb and finger. This is a great way to set the foundation for dexterity development in your fingers.

Tritone Publishing © 2025

Summary
Chapter 2

In Chapter 2, we learn about tuning the guitar and holding the guitar pick. Two very important fundamental principles of playing the guitar. That is why we learn about it so early in the training.

We first look at tuning the guitar. To do this correctly, we need to know the names of the strings, which we learned in lesson 3. Remember, you have 6 strings and 6 numbers, and the biggest number is the thickest string, and the smallest number is the thinnest string.

We then learn about the clip-on tuner, which is a great device for tuning the guitar. It's small and portable, clips nicely onto the headstock, and has a big display so we can easily see the string name we are tuning.

We then learn about another cool device called the guitar pick. This device helps you to get a more pronounced sound when strumming across the strings. We also learn that there are different ones to choose from, and it is held between the thumb and first finger.

We also learned that if we practice daily with a pick, it will help us to develop an articulate percussive attack, which will help to give a brighter sound. As well as help to build finger dexterity that will benefit our guitar playing in other ways to come.

Chapter 3

Reading Notation

Lesson 5: Chord charts

The most common notation for the guitar is chord charts. These are box diagrams that allow you to see the shape of the chord, and where you need to place your fingers on the fretboard.

Chord chart example:

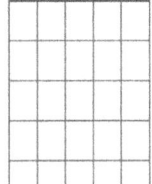 This diagram shows the guitar fretboard facing upward. The 6 vertical lines represent the strings (thickest to the left), and the 5 horizontal lines represent the nut and the first 5 frets. Chords will be indicated by dots on the strings.

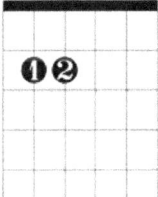 The **E minor chord** chart. The dots indicate that you place your fingers on the 2nd fret of the 5th & 4th strings. The numbers indicate which fingers to use. In this case, you will use the 1st and 2nd fingers.

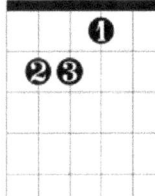 The **E major chord.** Can you see how it just adds one more finger? If you were to play the E minor with your two middle fingers, you could just add your index finger to play the E major chord. See how easy that would be?

Lesson 5 con't

Here are some benefits of being able to read chord charts:

- **Facilitates quicker learning:**

Reading chord charts can allow you to learn songs quicker. By being able to recognize the chords in a song, you can play it without previous rehearsal.

- **Develops sight reading skills:**

Being able to read music can be a huge benefit in playing the guitar, as it quickly gives you insights to a song you would not learn otherwise.

- **Enhances memory retention:**

Reading chord charts allows you to practice the skill of visualization. When you can see the chord in this manner, you retain it better.

- **Encourage creativity:**

When a guitarist can read chord charts, they can begin to create charts and progressions that fuel compositions of their own. This encourages creativity.

- **Boosts confidence:**

Since reading chord charts can allow you to quickly learn songs without previous rehearsal, it boosts your confidence. This allowing you to progess along your musical journey with more determination.

Tritone Publishing © 2025

Lesson 6: Reading guitar tabs

The other type of notation that you want to get familiar with is reading guitar tabs. Tabs is short for tablature. A form of notation specifically designed for fretted instruments. Aside from chord charts, this is the most common way that most guitarists read sheet music.

Unlike traditional sheet music, which uses staff lines for writing symbols on the lines and spaces in between them, guitar tabs use lines that represent the guitar strings, and numbers are placed upon them to indicate which fret along the fretboard to place your fingers on.

 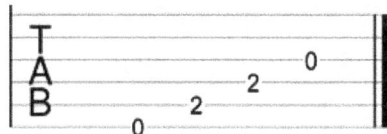

As you can see from the image above, we have six lines. These represent the six strings. Numbers are placed upon them to indicate the frets to play. Zero means the string is played open with no finger on it.

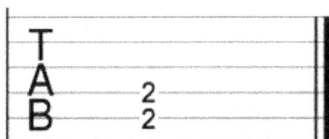

Here is the **Em chord** written in tab format. It is the same as the chord chart you learned earlier, just written horizontally instead of vertically.

**When reading tabs, you want to make sure to remember that your biggest string is on the bottom. The reason for this is that in notation, the lowest note is always on the bottom.

Lesson 6 con't

Guitar tabs can also work for single-note melody lines as well as for chords. Here are a few examples:

Example #1: All notes played on the 6th string

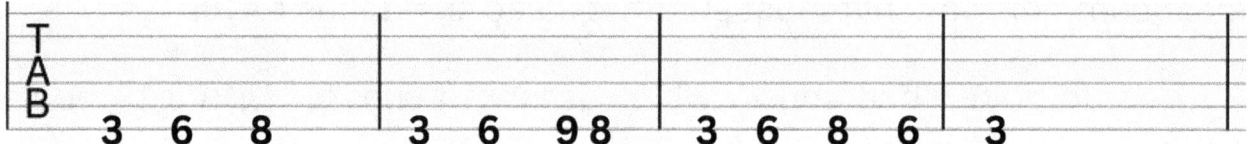

Example #2: All notes played on the 5th string

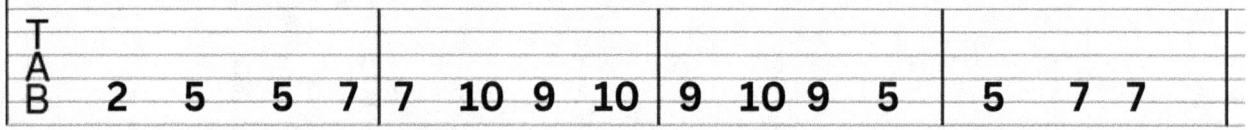

Example #3 All notes played on the 4th, 5th, & 6th strings

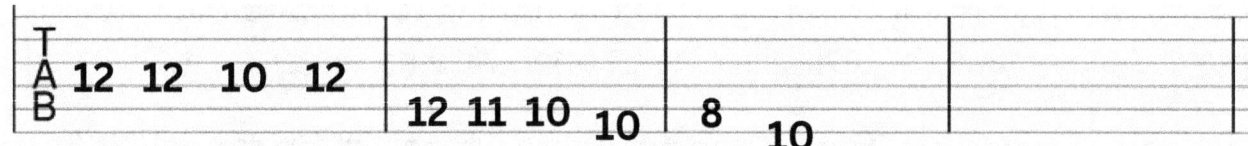

Here are a few more chords that are written in guitar tab.

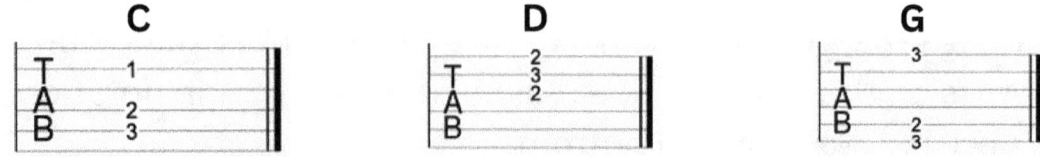

Tritone Publishing © 2025

Summary
Chapter 3

In Chapter 3, we learn about reading notation. The two most common types that relate to guitar playing. Chord charts and guitar tabs. By learning to read these two types of notation, you will be able to learn faster and retain information better.

Chord charts are simple diagrams that represent the guitar fretboard facing upward showing the first few frets. This is helpful for our uses here, because all the chords we will be playing ae in these first few freta.

Vertical lines represent the guitar strings, and vertical lines represent the frets. Dots are then placed on the vertical lines at various fret positions to tell us where to place our fingers. This is very useful for learning and playing chords to a song quickly.

Next, we have guitar tabs. These are especially helpful when playing melody lines and music further up the fretboard. These use only horizontal lines that represent the guitar strings the way you would play them. But, instead of dots placed on the lines, you have numbers.

Both of these two types of notation are very helpful in learning to play guitar, and if we learn to read and write in both formats. It will help our guitar playing tremendously.

Chapter 4
Forming Basic Chords

Lesson 7: Major chords

When it comes to guitar chords, there are thousands to choose from. I know, crazy, huh? We don't need to learn thousands of chords, we just need to learn the most common ones to get started. These are the major chords because they produce a nice, bright, happy sound.

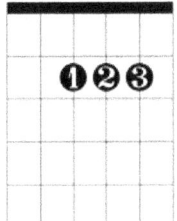

A major: This chord uses three fingers on the 2nd, 3rd, and 4th strings of the second fret. As I mentioned before, the numbers indicate which fingers to use when forming this chord. I suggest trying different fingers as well.

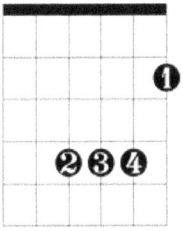

B major: As you can see, this chord is very similar to A major. You just move up two frets and place a finger on the 1st string second fret. You can use all 4 fingers as the diagram suggests or bar the three notes with one finger.

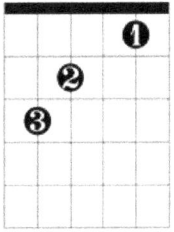

C major: This chord spans across the fretboard, skipping a string. It will require you to spread your fingers out a bit, but it is one of the most useful chords of the bunch. So be sure to learn it and learn it well.

Lesson 7 con't

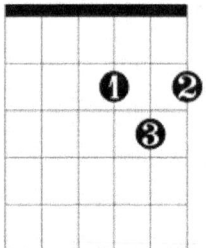
D major: This chord is played on the 1st, 2nd, & 3rd strings on the second and third frets. I recommend you work on switching from the C major chord to the D major chord, as this is a very popular transition in many songs.

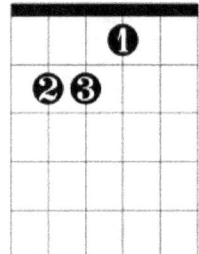
E major: If you look at the E minor you learned earlier, you'll see that this chord is very similar. You just need to add one note on the 3rd string of the first fret. You'll learn in the next lesson how this chord is similar to the A minor.

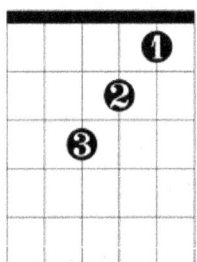
F major: This is a great chord to learn because it is almost the same as the C major chord. Being so, it makes a great chord to transition into. Once you have a C major down, try switching to the F major.

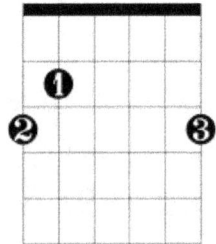
G major: This chord can be a bit tricky. The reason for this is that it spans across all six strings. You will need to put in some time with this chord. But it will be well worth it as it is found in many, many popular songs.

*****When forming these chords, work at playing on your fingertips.**

Tritone Publishing © 2025

Lesson 8: Minor chords

Now, let's take a look at some common minor chords that are used in a wide variety of songs. Later in the training, I'll teach why some are called major and some minor. But for now, just learn to form the chord shapes.

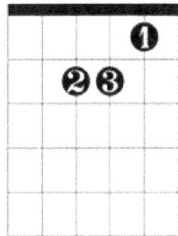

A minor: This is the counterpart to A major. Can you see that all you need to do is move one note over a fret from the major to create this chord? This is another popular chord you will find in many, many songs.

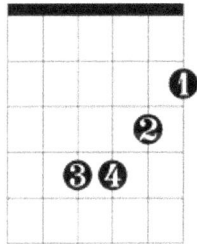

B minor: Once again, if you look at the B major chord, you will notice that all you need to do to form this chord is move over a note. I recommend practicing switching from B major to B minor.

Minor chords produce a sad sound compared to the bright, happy sound of the major chords. Listen for this as you form and play them.

Tritone Publishing © 2025

Lesson 8 con't

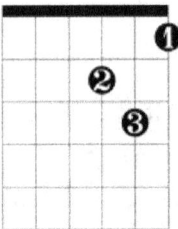

D minor: This is another chord that requires you to just move a note over a fret from its major counterpart. The only thing is, you'll need to reposition your fingers to do so. I recommend practicing this daily.

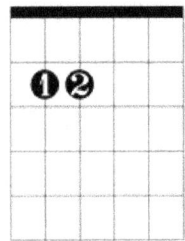

E minor: This is the chord that you first learned earlier in the training. This is the easiest chord of these to play, as it only requires two fingers. A great chord and is also found in many, many popular songs.

If you noticed, I didn't include **C minor**, **F minor**, or **G minor**. It's not that these chords do not exist, it's just that they are not as common in this format. Since this is a beginner course, it is best to stick to chords that are easiest to form and most common to play.

Also, notice that I only presented these in chord chart format. I did this because this is the easiest way to get started reading and forming guitar chords. Later, I will present them in guitar tabs as well. This way, you can learn both formats.

Summary
Chapter 4

In Chapter 4, we learned about forming basic chords. We learned that there are thousands of chords to choose from, but we don't need to learn them all, just the most common ones in songs. These will be the major and minor chords. In lesson 7, we'll start with the major chords.

Major chords are great because they produce a nice, bright, happy sound. So they are soothing to the ear. In this lesson, we learn 7 major chords to start with. A major, B major, C major, D major, e major, F major, and G major.

These are all presented in chord charts because that is the most common way we will come across them in guitar notation. S, learning them this way is highly beneficial.

We then look at minor chords. These are the counterpart to the major. These produce a sad moody sound and are very common in many songs as well. In lesson 8 we learn the A minor, B minor, D minor, and E minor.

C minor, F minor, and G minor are not included because they are not as common at this stage. Since this is a beginner course, we shall stick to chords that are easiest to form, most common to play, and found in hundreds of songs.

Remember, when forming these chords, play on your fingertips.

Chapter 5
Establishing Rhythm

Lesson 9: Strumming chords

Strumming is where you sweep the pick across the strings to create music with the chords we learned. This will be done in a down and upward motion.

Let's explore some basic strumming patterns that will get you started and make your chords sound like music.

Strumming pattern #1: Strum down.

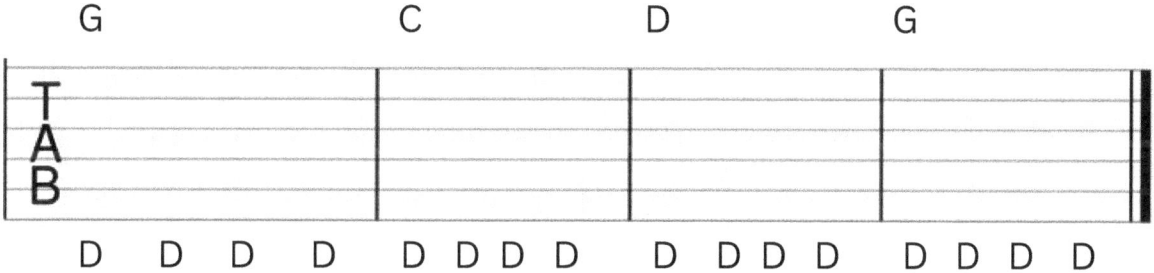

In the above example, you strum downward across all six strings 4 times on each chord. Keep a slow, steady pace and count as you proceed.

This may seem a bit akward at first, but don't worry, you are now developing your picking hand. Just take it slow one step at a time.

Lesson 9 con't

Strumming pattern #2: Down & back up.

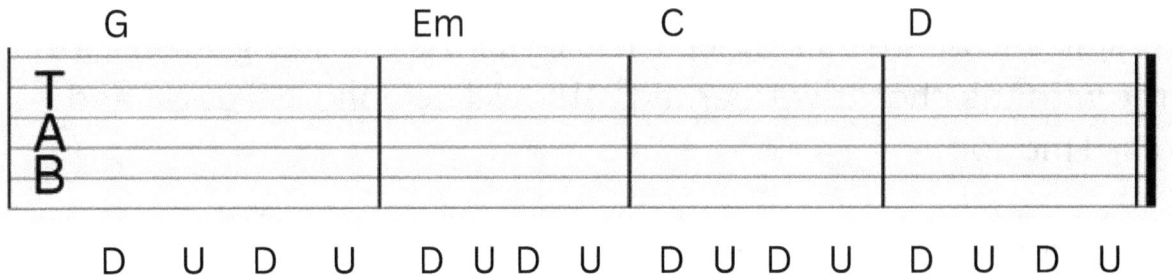

In this example, you strum down and then back up. As you do, this will give it a different rhythm. Keep it slow and steady as you do.

Strumming pattern #3: Down-up-down.

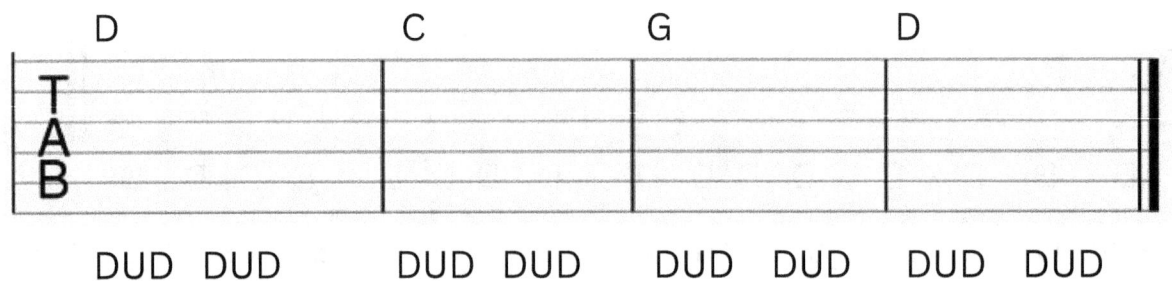

In this example, you strum three beats together as one to create a different type of rhythm. Try to keep a steady beat in the process.

Lesson 10: Develop proper timing

Besides strumming chords, you want to develop proper timing. This is how you create rhythm. It is not enough to just strum chords, you want to do it in such a way that it sounds musical.

Timing sequence #1: quarter note

Timing sequence #2: Eight note

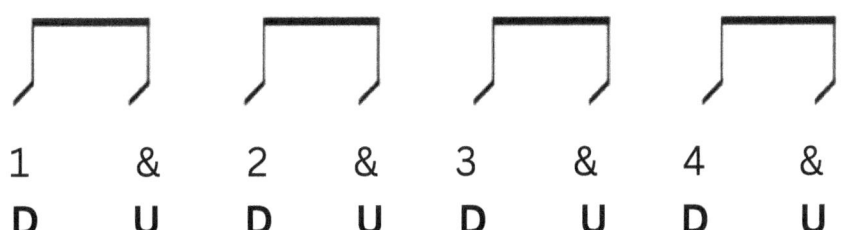

In these examples, we use quarter and eighth note strum patterns as the last lesson, but this time we add timing. Make sure to count while going through these.

Lesson 10 con't

Now, let's combine them to create rhythm patterns that are even more interesting.

Timing sequence #3: 2 quarter & 2 eighth

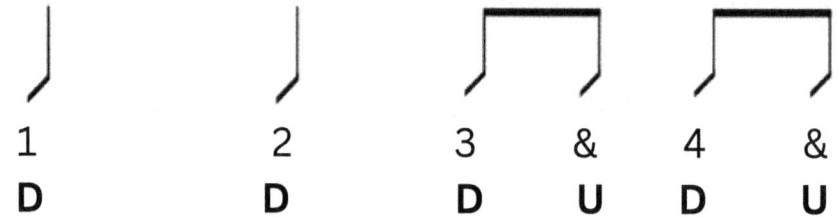

```
1      2      3   &   4   &
D      D      D   U   D   U
```

Timing sequence #4: 1 quarter & 3 eighth

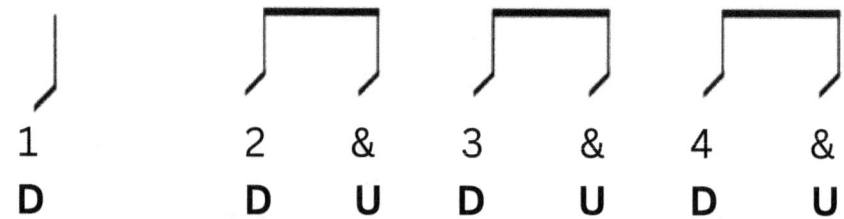

```
1      2   &   3   &   4   &
D      D   U   D   U   D   U
```

Can you see how this simple concept can create different rhythms while you strum chords? See if you can get creative and work out even more combinations of these timing sequences.

Summary
Chapter 5

In Chapter 5, we learned about how to establish rhythm. We will do this by strumming chords and developing proper timing. This will develop our picking hand and bring the chords that we've learned to life.

First, we look at strumming chords. This is where you sweep the pick across the strings to create music and is done with an up-and-down motion.

We explore 3 common strumming patterns. Strumming downward. Strum across all six strings 4 times per chord. We then look at strumming down and back up again. Finally, we look at combining these two techniques.

In lesson 10, we learn about different time sequences to help develop timing. Strumming is not enough. We need to do it in time. We learn about the quarter note, which is one beat and counted as 1, and then the eighth note counted as 1 and.

We then look at how we can combine these time sequences to create additional rhythms. First, we have 2 quarter notes and 2 eighth notes. Which gives a count of 1, 2, 3 & 4 &.

Then we have a rhythm sequence with 1 quarter note and 3 eighth notes which gives us a count of 1 2 & 3 & 4 &.

Tritone Publishing © 2025

Chapter 6
Chord Transisitons

Lesson 11: Changes chords smoothly

One of the things that will take some time at the beginning of your guitar-playing journey will be practicing chord changes. Moving smoothly between chords is the goal, and this can only be done through daily application.

I recommend you start with switching between two chords at a time. Once you get this down, add three and four. Once you get that down, speed up the process.

Chord switch #1:

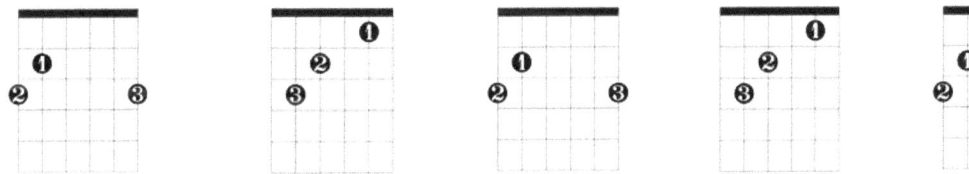

These two chords are probably the most common. They are presented in many, many popular songs. If it has a C major in it, it more than likely has a G major in it as well. Work on switching between these smoothly.

Lesson 11 con't

Chord switch #2:

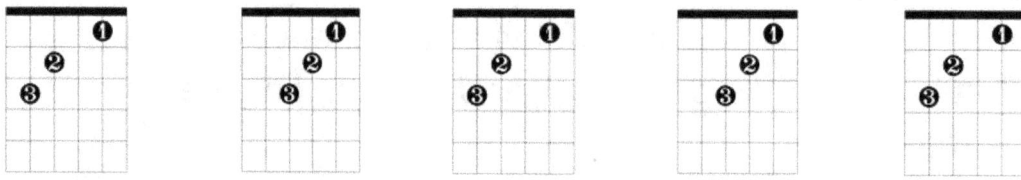

The chords C major to F major are great chord changes also.

Chord switch #3:

The A minor and D major are also common chord changes.

Chord switch #4:

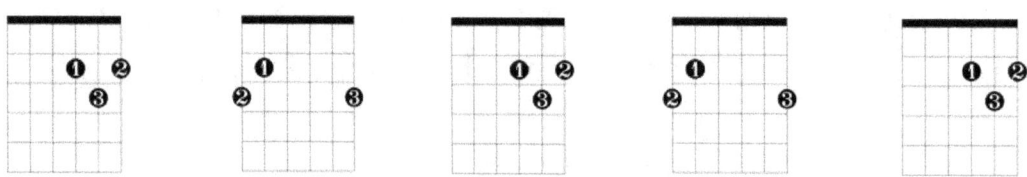

Get this last switch down, and you'll be gold.

Tritone Publishing © 2025

Lesson 12: Building muscle memory

As I said earlier, switching chords in the beginning is not easy. You will need to build up your muscle memory, and this can only be done through daily practice. The good side is that any growing pains you experience were also experienced by your favorite players.

Everybody goes through it, and I do mean everybody! There are no exceptions to the rule. So the sooner you get to work on it, the sooner you can get to the fun part of playing songs.

This will need to be accomplished with both hands. Building motor skills and hand-to-hand coordination is what the fundamentals are all about. Master these, and they will serve you well for years to come.

Here are a few training tips:

Practice slowly:
- Practice all techniques learned so far, slowly and accurately. This will give your muscles time to develop.

Music is a language:
- Remember also that music is a language, so this means the mind needs time to develop as well.

Lesson 12 con't

Training tips continued:

Devlop patience:
- You must develop patience and be consistent with your efforts. When it comes to accomplishment, consistency is everything.

Short intervals:
- In the beginning, practice in short intervals to allow the mind and body to process the new information and techniques being learned.

Start simple:
- Always start your practice sessions with something simple. That way, your muscles have time to warm up.

Practice daily:
- The importance of daily practice cannot be emphasized enough. This is where you will develop all your habits. Good or bad.

If you follow these training tips regularly, I guarantee that you will see great results over time. Remember, you are doing something new and there will be a learning curve. Have patience going through it, and you will come out a winner.

Summary
Chapter 6

In Chapter 6, we learned about chord transitions. The goal is to move smoothly through chord changes, which can only be achieved through daily application. The best way to accomplish this is by switching between two chords.

Lesson 11 goes through 4 chord switches. The first one is between the chords G and C. The second is between the chords C and F. The third is between the chords Am and D., and the fourth is between D and G. All these chords can be found in many popular songs.

We then look at tips on how to build muscle memory. This can help with switching chords faster and more smoothly. The reason why these tips are important to pay attention to is that at the beginning of our journey, we will experience growing pains.

No need to worry though because everyone goes through it. Building motor skills and hand-to-hand coordination is what the fundamental principles are all about. Make sure to do such things as, practice slowly, develop patience, start simple, and work at these daily.

Remember, the hardest part of our guitar-playing journey is at the start. This is where the most work is necessary. Developing the proper skills to sound great on the instrument. Do this properly, and these skills will last us a lifetime.

Tritone Publishing © 2025

Chapter 7
More Common Chords

Lesson 13: 7th chords

Other chords that are popular in songs and not too difficult to form are 7th chords. Learn these and add them to your chord vocabulary.

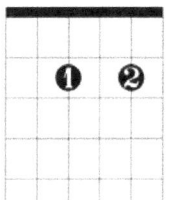
The A7 chord. Notice how similar it is to A major. Just take off the middle note, and you've got a new chord.

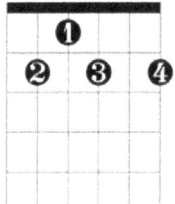
The B7 chord. This chord is a bit different from its major and minor counterparts, but not too difficult to form.

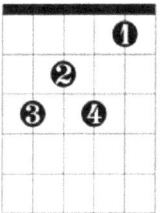
The C7 chord. If you look at the infamous C major chord, you can see that all you need to do is add a note to form this one.

Tritone Publishing © 2025

Lesson 13th con't

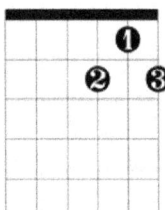 **The D7 chord.** If you look at the D major, this chord is the same, just reversed. So not too hard to form.

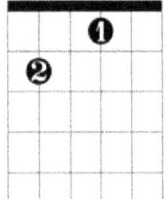 **The E7 chord.** This is another chord that, if you look at its major counterpart, you just take a note away to form it.

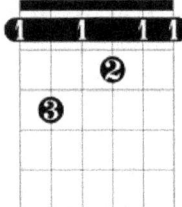 **The F7 chord.** This one is a bit odd because you bar across all six strings with your index finger to form it.

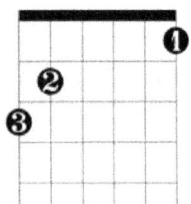 **The G7 chord.** This chord is similar to the G major, except you move the note on the 1st string over two frets.

Tritone Publishing © 2025

Lesson 14: Additional chords

Here are a few more chords that are common in a lot of songs. Later in the training I'll explain why they are named as such.

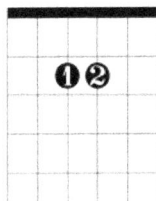

The Asus2 chord. As you can see, this chor is similar to the A major; you just take away a note.

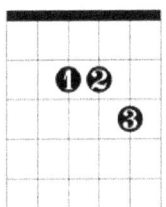

The Asus4 chord. In this example, you take the note on the 2nd string and move it forward by one fret.

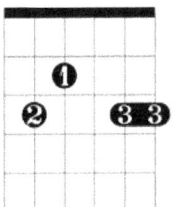

The Cadd9 chord. This chord is a bit odd as well, but it is found in many popular songs.

Tritone Publishing © 2025

Lesson 14 con't

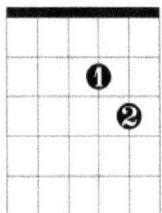 **The Dsus2 chord.** In this chord, you just take your finger off of the 1st string to create it.

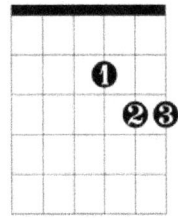 **The Dsus4 chord.** Notice how you take the D major and move a note forward to create this chord.

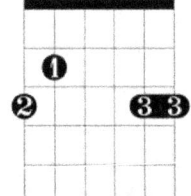 **The alternate G chord.** This is a G major chord, except with an added note. Works great with the Cadd9 chord.

All these chords have weird names but are all very common in many songs. That is why I included them. Don't worry about the names for now; just learn to play them and add them to your chord vocabulary.

Summary
Chapter 7

In Chapter 7, we learned the 7th chord. These are chords that are also very popular in many songs and not too hard to play as well. In lesson 13, we learn 7 of these types of chords. The A7, B7, C7, D7, E7, F7, and G7.

It is also a good idea to take note of the F7 chord. This chord uses what's called a bar in it. This is where you use your index finger to bar across all 6 strings to form the chord. This is called a barre chord.

Since this is a beginner course we won't go into these types of chords because they are much harder to form. But I added it in the lesson just to give you a glimpse into them. Once we get the basics down, we can move on to more complex chords like these types.

In the next lesson, we look at additional chords. These are chords that have weird names but are easy to form and also popular in many, many great songs.

Such chords as Asus2, Asus4, Dsus2, Dsus4, Cadd9, and G alt. are all great chords found in many songs and not too hard to play. The G chord in this lesson is presented because it's a great switch to the Cadd9 chord.

For now, don't worry about their names; just worry about forming them and adding them to your chord vocabulary.

Chapter 8
Capo & Fingerstyle

Lesson 15: Using a capo

Another very popular tool for playing acoustic guitar is the capo. This small device clamps on the guitar's neck, shortening the string length and affecting the pitch. This allows you to play further up the neck in different positions without changing chord shapes.

Capo examples:

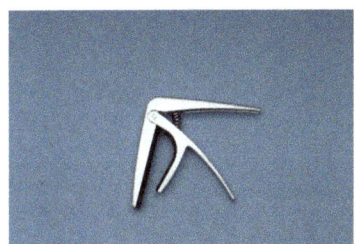

Notice how this device has a spring to keep it clamped on the guitar neck.

This example shows how the capo looks clamped on the guitar neck. Acting as a moveable nut, the capo allows you to move up the fretboard.

This can be very useful when playing in different keys or when more complex chords need to be simplified.

Tritone Publishing © 2025

Lesson 15 con't

In this up-close picture, we have the capo clamped to the neck from a different point of view. With it being moveable, keys can be changed in an instant.

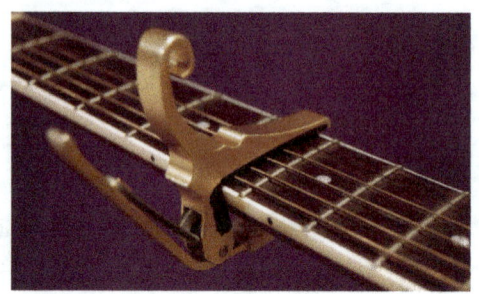

In this picture, you can see how the capo is used in action. It is clamped on the first fret while forming an A minor chord. You just play like you normally would.

In this picture, the capo is placed further up the fretboard on the 4th fret. This shows an example of how the capo can be played in different positions.

As you can see, the capo is a cool little tool. I recommend you get one, put it on your guitar, and play with it. Try it out in different positions while going through your chords. You might get inspired.

Lesson 16: Using your fingers

Besides strumming the chords with a pick, you can also play them with your fingers. This technique is called fingerstyle or it is sometimes called finger picking.

As you can see from this picture, you will position your hand so you can play all the strings with your thumb and fingers.

This will allow you to play the notes of the chords individually, instead of all together like when you strum them.

In this chapter, we are going to look at a few simple picking exercises to help you develop this style of playing. This will allow you to expand your guitar-playing skills and song repertoire.

Here is a close-up picture of the picking hand. Traditionally, your thumb will play the top 3 strings and your fingers will play the bottom 3.

Tritone Publishing © 2025

lesson 16 con't

Finger exercise #1:

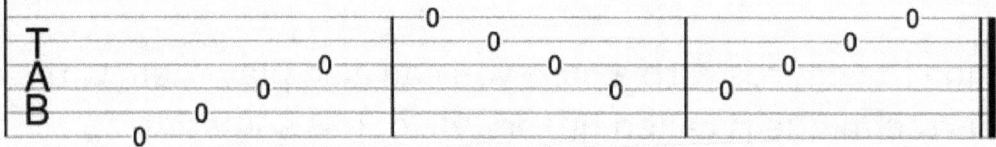

Play the 6th, 5th & 4th strings with your thumb and the others with your fingers.

Finger exercise #2:

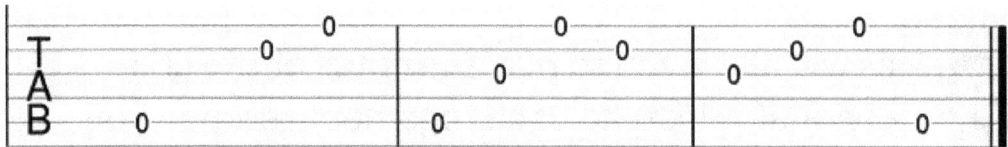

Play the 5th string with your thumb and the 2nd and 1st strings with your fingers.

Finger exercise #3:

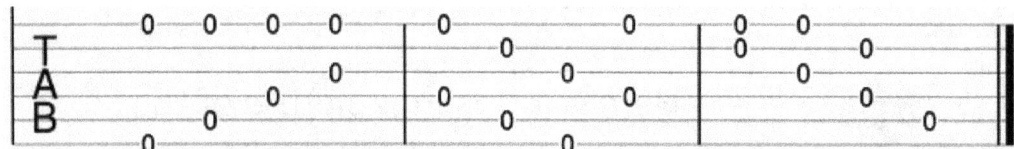

This example is a little advanced. Here, you play two strings at a time with both your thumb and finger, except for the last note.

Summary
Chapter 8

In Chapter 8, we learn about using two more things that can add to our guitar playing. First, in lesson 15 we learn about the capo. A very cool little device that allows us to play our chords further up the neck.

Since the chords we learned have strings in them that are note fretted, they need to be played in their normal position. If we were to try to play them further up the fretboard they wouldn't sound right. This is where the capo comes.

The capo is also useful for changing the key that we play in. When we clamp the capo on the guitar neck, it shortens the strings. This raises the pitch of the strings. Musical keys like the key of A major, for instance, are based on pitch. The capo allows us to extend this.

The next thing we learn in this chapter is that in addition to strumming with a pick, we can also play with our fingers. This style of playing allows us to play the notes of the chords individually. This gives us a softer, more subtle sound.

To be able to master this technique, we need to have our fingers in a certain position. The thumb plays the top low strings, and the fingers play the bottom high strings. Playing finger exercise patterns daily will help develop our fingers to do this.

Chapter 9

Basic Music Theory

Lesson 17: Notes on the fretboard

When it comes to learning music theory, it starts with the 12 notes of the musical alphabet. A-G#. This is also called the chromatic scale. This means, that all the notes reside right next to each other.

Music alphabet: A A# B C C# D D# E F F# G G#

If you notice, all the notes have a # after them except for two. The B and the E. Remember this. All 12 notes will reside on each string.

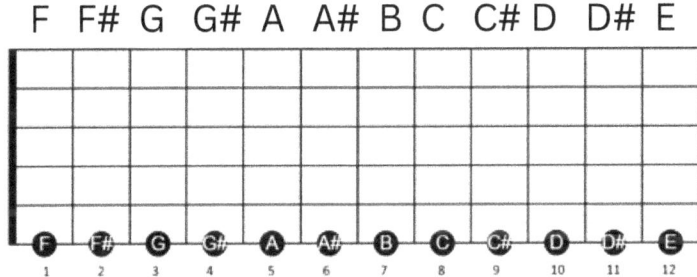

The **Low E string**. The string by itself will be the E note, and then it will proceed from there. Notes will repeat after the 12th fret.

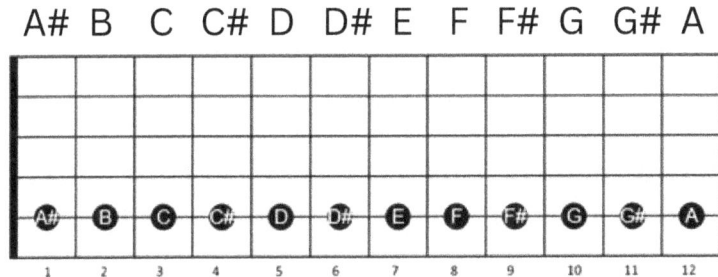

The **A string**. The string by itself will be the A note, and then it will proceed from there. Notes will repeat after the 12th fret.

Tritone Publishing © 2025

50 Lesson 17 con't

The D string. The string by itself will be the D note, and then it will proceed from there. Notes will repeat after the 12th fret.

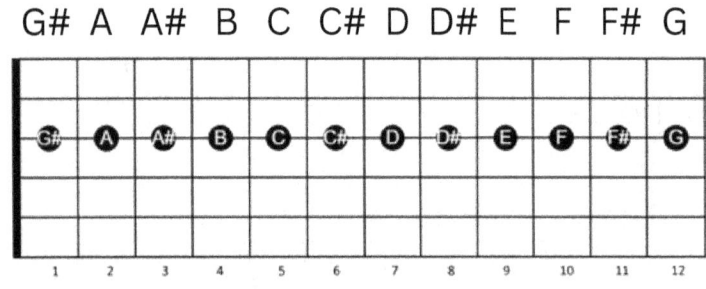

The G string. The string by itself will be the G note, and then it will proceed from there. Notes will repeat after the 12th fret.

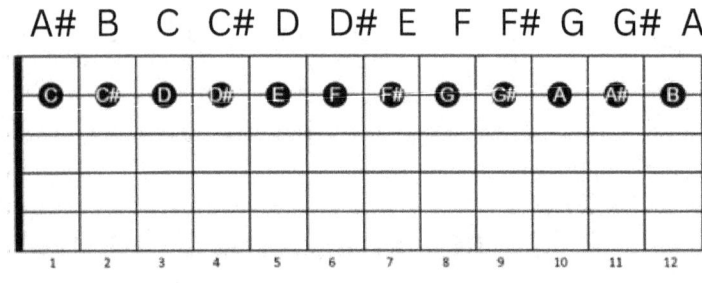

The B string. The string by itself will be the B note, and then it will proceed from there. Notes will repeat after the 12th fret.

** I didn't add the high E string because the notes are the same as the notes on the low E string.

Tritone Publishing © 2025

Lesson 18: Chord construction

In the previous lesson, I showed you all the notes on the fretboard. I recommend you go through these daily until you memorize them. They will come in handy for this lesson on chord construction. As well as any other lesson you might study further down the line on music theory.

Out of the 12 notes of the music alphabet, we take 7 to create the major scale. This major scale will be the foundation for all chords and other scales you might learn in the future.

Here is an example:

C major: C D E F G A B. These particular notes are chosen because the scale must have the Do Re Mi sound for it to be diatonically correct. All major scale notes in all keys will be chosen because of this concept.

Now that we know the notes, we can give each one a number value.

C D E F G A B
1 2 3 4 5 6 7

It is these 7 notes in the C major scale, that the C major chord will be created out of. All chords have a note formula that comes from the notes of the key they come out of.

Lesson 18 con't

All chords learned so far can be created from the notes of the keys they come out of. The keys of A major, B major, C major, D major, etc. These are created by using 3 notes. The 1st, the 3rd, and the 5th notes.

A major: A B C# D E F# G#
　　　　　　1 2 3   4 5 6   7

A major chord: 1 3 5.　**A minor chord**: 1 b3 5　**A7**: 1 3 5 b7
　　　　　　　　A C# E　　　　　　　　　　A C E　　　　　A C# E G

Can you see how these chords are created out of the notes within the key? In the case of the minor and the 7th chord, we flatten the 3rd and the 7th note. With this concept, we could create an Am7th by adding the flat 7th note to the minor chord. This is the science of music.

D major: D E F# G A B C#
　　　　　　1 2 3   4 5 6 7

D major: 1 3 5.　**D minor**: 1 b3 5　**Dsus 2:** 1 2 5　**Dsus4**: 1 4 5
　　　　　D F# A　　　　　　　　D F A　　　　　　D E A　　　　　　D G A

See how this concept works the same way? If you check the notes of the chords you've learned so far, you'll see they are constructed from these notes. If you want to create chords on the fly, you need to know your notes.

Summary
Chapter 9

In Chapter 9, we learn a little bit about music theory. This covers notes on the fretboard, and chord construction. When it comes to learning music theory, it all comes down to the 12 notes of the musical alphabet. Or sometimes called the chromatic scale.

These 12 notes will be A A# B C C# D D# E F F# G and G#. These are the notes that are in music styles like Jazz, Country, Blues, Pop, Rock, etc. They are also found on each of the 6 guitar strings. Knowing where these notes are on each string will allow us to create chords on the fly by mastering the fretboard.

Lesson 17 goes through the notes on each string, and we learn that the notes always follow the same order. We just start on the note that the string is associated with. If it is the D string, we start with the D note and proceed from there.

Next, in lesson 18, we learn that we take 7 notes out of the 12 to create a key like C major. Out of these 7 notes, we can create chords like majors, minors, and the 7th chord. This is the science of music. Each chord has a specific note formula.

By learning about these note formulas and knowing the notes that are in specific keys, we can create a wide variety of chords. Not just the ones that we have learned.

Tritone Publishing © 2025

Chapter 10

Additional Training

Lesson 19: Ear Training

In addition to being able to read chord charts and guitar tabs, you also want to work on developing your ear. This is done through ear training.

The ability to hear something and immediately transfer it ot the guitar is what playing by ear is, and it is a very popular way to approch the instrument.

This way takes time to master, but can be done. In this lesson, we will look at some tips that can help you develop your ear to approach the guitar in this universal method.

Ear Training Tips

- **Focus on the root:**

The root note of most chords is the lowest note. In the lesson on basic theory, this would be the 1 of the 1 3 5 formula. Focus on listening for this note in the chords as you play them.

- **Identify notes:**

Once you have the root note down, work at identifying the other 2 notes in the chord. This will help you to hear what chord is being played in a song.

- **Use your voice**

When learning to play the guitar, your objective is to make a connection with the instrument. One of the best ways to do this is to add your voice. Learn to sing.

- **Identify intervals:**

If you add your voice, it can help you to identify note intervals. This is the distance between notes. This ability will help you pick out solos and melody lines.

- **Practice daily:**

Last but not least, you need to practice daily. To develop playing by ear, you need to spend quality time with your guitar. The more you are committed to the instrument, the better your ear will develop.

The ability to play by ear is a great way to approach the instrument as it eliminates the need to read sheet music. But you must have patience and persistence because it does take time to develop. Put in the effort and overtime, you will see results.

Lesson 20: Practice habits

This lesson right here is the one that's going to make all the difference in your guitar playing. Developing practice habits. Quality practice habits will keep you motivated and on track to your goal of becoming a great guitar player.

Habits to Practice for Best Performance:

- **Set a goal:**

The best way to stay on track is to set a goal of what you want to accomplish with your guitar playing. Why are you taking the time to learn? What are you hoping to accomplish?

- **Track your progress:**

Once you have your goal set, you can then begin to track your progress. This is important as it will indicate where you are and how far you still need to go.

- **Know your chords:**

Make sure you know all your chords. Write them down if necessary. The better you know them and the faster you can switch between them, the better you will be.

Lesson 20 con't

- **Read notation:**

Make sure to practice reading your chord charts and guitar tabs. These can come in handy when you come across a song you like and can read the chords.

- **Timing:**

This is a skill that is a must to master. I can't begin to tell you how many guitarists I've run into over the years who don't get this lesson. Work on it daily, and it will pay huge dividends.

- **Know your notes::**

If you'd like to know about chord construction and other things that have to do with music theory, make sure to know your notes. Master the fretboard and create chords quickly.

- **Have fun:**

Last but not least, have fun with your learning. Don't let it become a chore. If you do, you won't stick with it. Take it one step at a time, and you will begin to see results, and that's when the real fun begins.

Summary
Chapter 10

In Chapter 10, we take a look at a couple more things that can help us to become great guitar players. Training our ears to recognize notes, and developing quality practice habits.

Playing guitar by ear is a very common way to approach the instrument. Many guitar players play this way. The benefit of this method is there is no need to rely on reading notation.

The ability to hear something and immediately transfer it to the guitar is a skill that takes hours of practice to develop. This is why we have learned some training tips to help with this endeavor.

In addition to training your ear, you want to take time and develop quality practice habits. These can make all the difference in whether you become good or great at playing the guitar.

A few tips to remember are to set a goal, track your progress, and focus on what you've learned and what you still need to work on, like knowing all your chords.

Be sure to work daily on reading notation, basic music theory, knowing your notes, and above all else, having fun learning. Remember, you don't want it to become a chore. Have fun with it, and it will show in your playing.

Tritone Publishing © 2025

Acoustic Quiz

Assess your learning

All answers are within the lessons. Find them there if you don't know the question. Good luck.

Q: What are the parts of the guitar?

A: _____

Q: What position is the guitar recommended to be played?

A: _____

Q: What device do you use to tune the guitar?

A: _____

Q: What is the benefit of using a guitar pick?

A: _____

Q: What are chord charts?

A: _____

Quiz Con't

Q: What are guitar tabs?

A: _____

Q: What kind of sound does a major chord produce?

A: _____

Q: What kind of sound does a minor chord produce?

A: _____

Q: What does it mean to strum chords?

A: _____

Q: What are quarter notes?

A: _____

Remember, this is just an assesment for you to check your progress and see what you still need to work on.

Quiz Con't

Q: What are eighth notes?

A: _____

Q: What is the time value of a quarter note?

A: _____

Q: What is the time value of an eighth note?

A: _____

Q: How many quarter notes are in timing sequence #1?

A: _____

Q: How many quarter notes are in timing sequence #4?

A: _____

Remember, if you don't know the answer, don't fret; just go to the lesson it's associated with and find it.

Quiz Con't

Q: Why is changing chords smoothly important?
A: _____

Q: What is the best way to build muscle memory?
A: _____

Q: How many 7th chords are presented in lesson 13?
A: _____

Q: What are some additional chords?
A: _____

Q: What is a capo and how does it work?
A: _____

Remember, writing is just as important as reading. It helps with memory retention and communication enhancement.

Quiz Con't

Q: What is the benefit of playing with your fingers?
A: _____

Q: What are the 12 notes of the music alphabet?
A: _____

Q: What is the note formula for the major and minor chords?
A: _____

Q: What does learning to play be ear accomplish?
A: _____

Q: Why are having good practice habits important?
A: _____

The more time you put into knowing the answers to all these questions, the better you will be able to express yourself on the guitar.

Conclusion

Acoustic Guitar 101

If you have made it this far I want to congratulate you. You have learned quite a bit about how to get started playing the acousitc guitar. Now, since this is only a beginner course, we haven't touched on all things acoustic, but we have enough to get you up and running.

If you learned all the lessons taught here in this training course, you should be able to strum chords with a pick, as well as play them with your fingers if you choose to do so.

You should be able to read simple notation in both chord charts and a little bit in tab format. You should now know all the notes on each string as well as how to recognize them in all the chords you've learned in this training.

You should have a basic understanding of music theory and how chords are constructed out of the notes in a key. How a major chord has a natural 3rd note as the minor chord has a flattened 3rd note, and the 7th chord is created by adding the flat 7 to the major.

These things and more that you have learned in this book will set you on a path to successful guitar playing. Of course, that will only be if you stay focused and practice daily. Good luck, and have fun!

Chord Reference
most commonly used

69

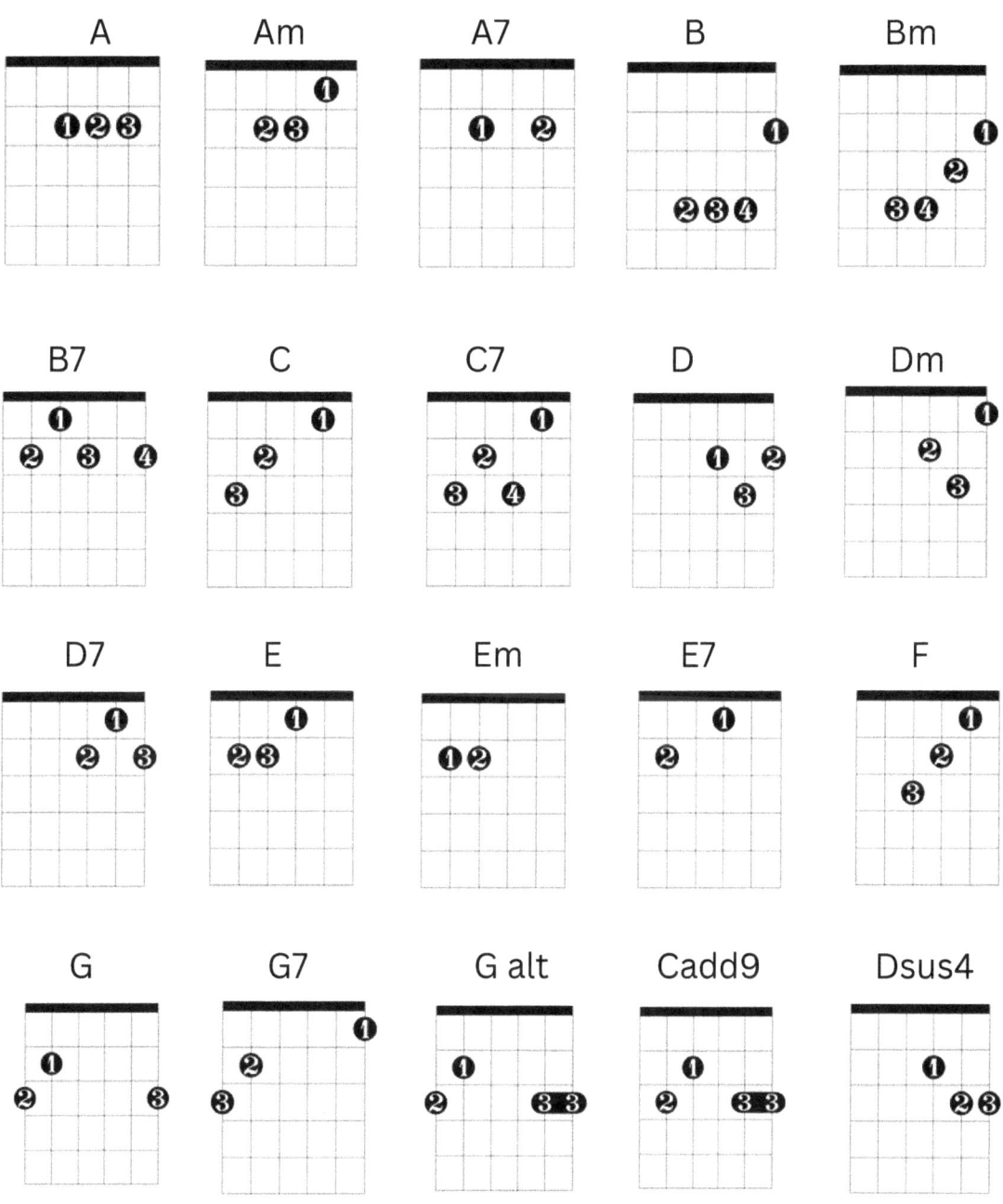

Tritone Publishing © 2025

Tritone Publishing © 2025

About The Author

DwaynesGuitarLessons.com

Dwayne Jenkins is a professional guitar teacher, an accomplished musician, and an entrepreneur. He has been learning, playing, and teaching guitar lessons throughout Denver, CO, for over two decades.

He is now bringing his special training skills and methodology that have been honed and hand-crafted throughout the years on how to play to students around the world.

Dwayne has a unique, exciting approach that gets students of all ages and skill levels enjoying the fun of playing guitar and ukulele. His enthusiasm and love for teaching shine through every lesson that he creates.

His lessons are designed to enhance your ability to progress. No matter your reason for learning, there will always be something in Dwayne's books and products to help you achieve your dreams.

So, if you're a student looking to start or a student looking to further your education, be sure to get involved with Dwayne's guitar lessons and learn why playing the guitar is one of the greatest things you can do for yourself.

Tritone Publishing © 2025

Tritone Publishing © 2025

Dive Deeper

Other Ttiles By Dwayne Jenkins

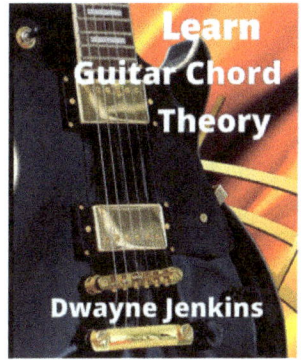

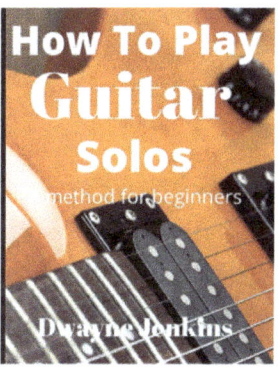

Al books can be found in paperback and digital format worldwide.

Tritone Publishing © 2025